From Seed to Daisy

Following the Life Cycle

by Laura Purdie Salas

illustrated by Jeff Yesh

PICTURE WINDOW BOOKS
Minneapolis, Minnesota

Thanks to our advisers for their expertise, research, and advice:

Kathryn Orvis, Ph.D., Associate Professor/Extension Specialist
Department of Youth Development & Agricultural Education
Purdue University, West Lafayette, Indiana

Terry Flaherty, Ph.D., Professor of English
Minnesota State University, Mankato

Editor: Shelly Lyons
Designers: Nathan Gassman and Lori Bye
Page Production: Melissa Kes
Associate Managing Editor: Christianne Jones
The illustrations in this book were created digitally.

Picture Window Books
151 Good Counsel Drive
P.O. Box 669
Mankato, MN 56002-0669
877-845-8392
www.picturewindowbooks.com

Photo Credits: © 2008 Jupiterimages Corporation, 23.

All books published by Picture Window Books
are manufactured with paper containing at least
10 percent post-consumer waste.

Library of Congress Cataloging-in-Publication Data
Salas, Laura Purdie.
From seed to daisy ; following the life cycle / by Laura Purdie Salas ;
illustrated by Jeff Yesh.
p. cm. — (Amazing science. Life cycle)
ISBN 978-1-4048-4919-8 (library binding)
1. Daisies—Life cycles—Juvenile literature. I. Yesh, Jeff, 1971- ill.
II. Title.
QK495.C74S24 2009
583'.99—dc22
2008006431

Table of Contents

Beautiful Blooms

Like animals, trees and other plants have a life cycle. Daisies are a common kind of plant in North America. There are many kinds of daisies. Let's take a look at the Shasta daisy.

The man who named the Shasta daisy thought the white petals looked like snow on Mount Shasta, in California.

The Way a Plant Begins

Flowering plants start out as seeds and grow to be plants. Then adult plants make seeds, and the cycle starts over.

A seed is like a treasure chest. Everything a Shasta daisy needs to start growing is already in the seed.

The yellow circle in the center of a Shasta daisy is a group of many tiny yellow flowers. The circular group of flowers is called a composite flower. When the daisy is dry and wilted, the seeds will come out of the tiny yellow flowers.

The Seedling

When conditions are right, a root starts to grow down from the Shasta daisy seed. Then a stem pushes upward through the dirt. The stem has two tiny leaves called seed leaves. This young plant is called a seedling.

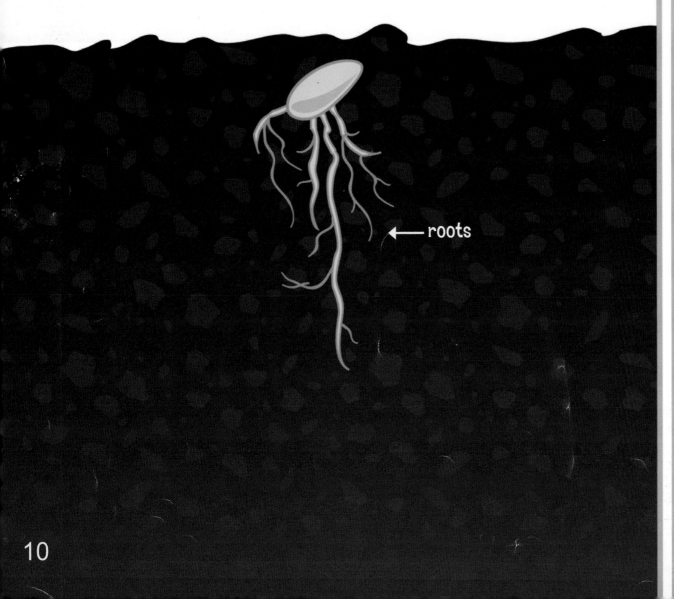

← roots

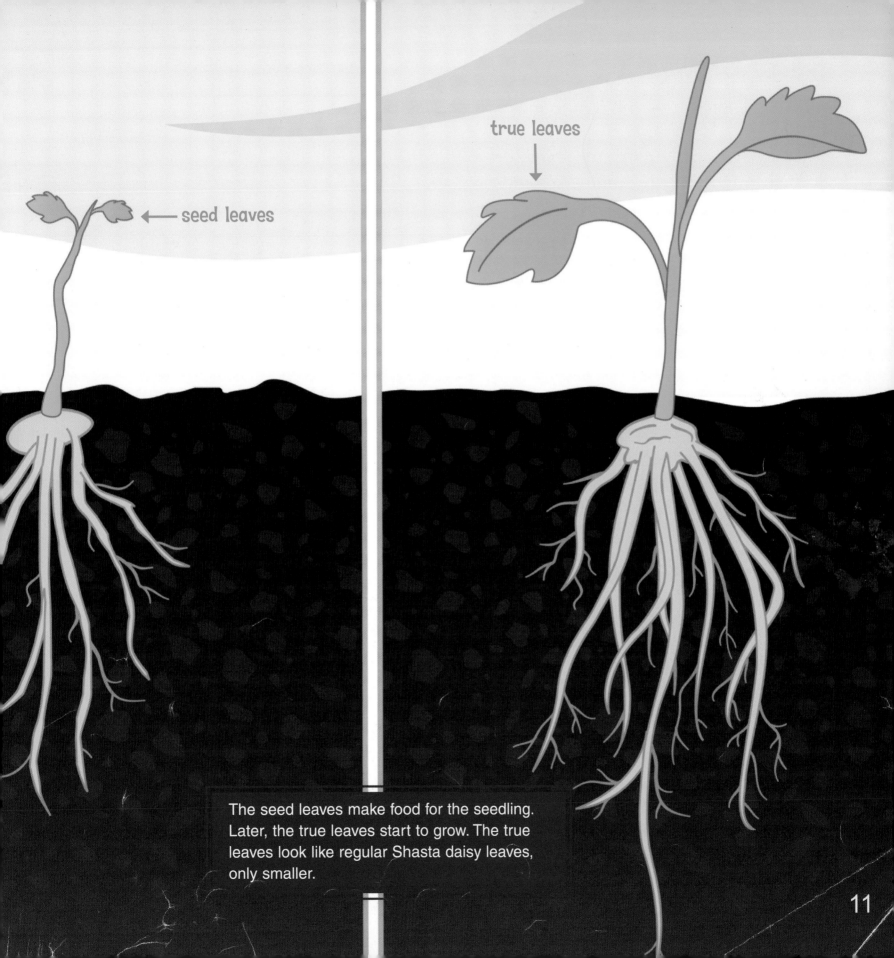

seed leaves

true leaves

The seed leaves make food for the seedling. Later, the true leaves start to grow. The true leaves look like regular Shasta daisy leaves, only smaller.

11

Time to Grow

Plants use energy from the sun to make food. This process is called photosynthesis.

Energy from the sun, along with water and food from the soil helps the daisy grow. A full-grown Shasta daisy plant is about 2 to 3 feet (61 to 91 centimeters) tall. It can be about 2 feet (61 cm) wide.

During photosynthesis, a plant turns light energy into chemical energy. The plant stores the chemical energy as sugars. It will use the sugars for food.

13

Stems and Flowers

Each Shasta daisy plant may have many stems and flowers. But Shasta daisies do not bloom during the first year of growth. After the first year, the flowers bloom each summer and into the fall. The plants do not grow in cool areas during winter.

Shasta daisies are perennial plants. This means they live three years or longer. Some kinds of flowers are annuals. That means they live just one year.

15

Pollination

A Shasta daisy's flowers contain male parts, the stamens, and a female part, the stigma. The stamens make a yellow powder called pollen. Pollen is needed to make new flowers.

The daisy's bright white petals attract insects such as bees and butterflies. The insects land on the small yellow flowers and drink the sweet liquid, or nectar, inside. When an insect lands on the flowers, pollen sticks to it. When the insect flies to the next flower, it carries the pollen along with it.

When pollen is moved from a stamen to a stigma, the flower is fertilized. Because Shasta daisy flowers have both male and female parts, they can fertilize themselves. They can also fertilize other daisies.

After Pollination

After pollination, a tiny seed grows inside each pollinated flower. The daisy flowers dry up. The white petals surrounding the flowers fall to the ground. Soon the seeds drop to the ground, too. Birds and other animals like to eat these seeds.

If you like to grow Shasta daisies, you can save the seeds and grow new Shasta daisy plants the following year.

19

Seeds on the Move

Daisy seeds need to travel away from their parent plant. This movement is called dispersal. Sometimes animals carry seeds away and drop them. Other times, animals eat the seeds. The seeds return to the ground in the animals' waste.

Wind and water can also carry seeds away. If a seed lands in a spot with good soil and lots of sunlight, a daisy will grow in spring.

You should plant Shasta daisies in a spot where they will receive plenty of sunlight. If a Shasta daisy does not get enough water, it will start to wilt. During dry times of summer, you should water Shasta daisy plants.

Life Cycle of a Shasta Daisy

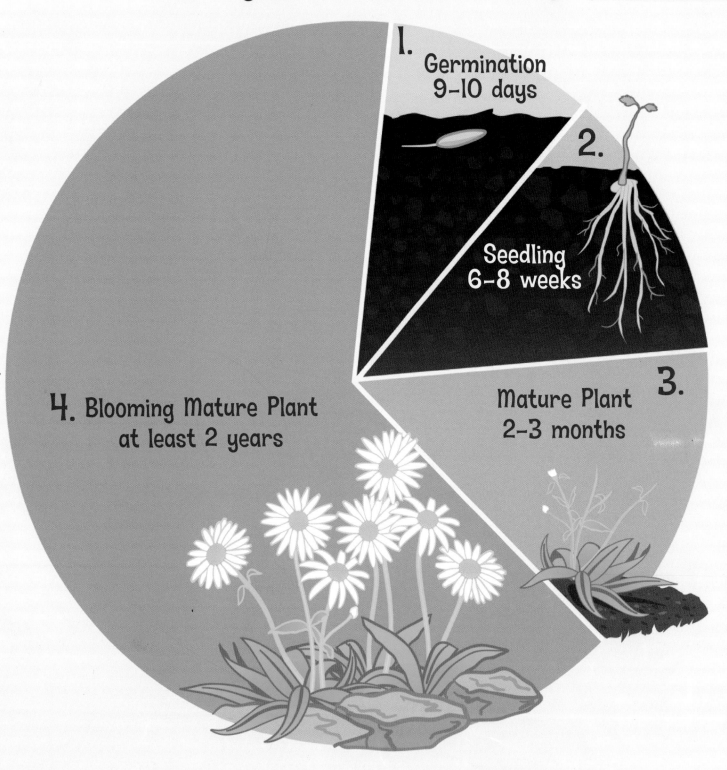

1. Germination 9-10 days

2. Seedling 6-8 weeks

3. Mature Plant 2-3 months

4. Blooming Mature Plant at least 2 years

Fun Facts

Shasta daisy in bloom

- A Shasta daisy looks dead during the winter. But its stems and roots live. It will grow new flowers the following summer.

- Many seeds stay inactive until all of the conditions are right. That's why seeds can be dispersed in the fall but not germinate until the following spring.

- There are many kinds of Shasta daisies, some of them are the Alaska, Snow Cap, and Silver Princess.

- Although the Shasta daisy can survive on little water, you should water the plant during especially dry times.

Glossary

annuals—flowering plants that live for just one summer

composite flower—one flower made of many tiny flowers

dispersal—the spreading of seeds

germination—when a seed begins to grow

perennial—a plant that lives for three or more years

photosynthesis—a process plants use to make food and oxygen

pollen—a powder made by flowers to help them create new seeds

pollination—the process of a female part of the flower receiving pollen

roots—the part of a plant that grows underground and soaks up water and nutrients

seed—the part of a flower that will grow into a new plant

seed coat—the outer layer of a seed

seedling—a young plant

stamen—the male part of the flower that makes pollen

stigma—the female part of the flower that makes seeds when pollinated

To Learn More

More Books to Read

Aloian, Molly, and Bobbie Kalman. *The Life Cycle of a Flower*. New York: Crabtree Pub. Co., 2004.

Aston, Dianna Hutts. *A Seed Is Sleepy*. San Francisco: Chronicle Books, 2007.

Blackaby, Susan. *Buds and Blossoms: A Book About Flowers*. Minneapolis: Picture Window Books, 2003.

Robbins, Ken. *Seeds*. New York: Atheneum Books for Young Readers, 2005.

On the Web

FactHound offers a safe, fun way to find Web sites related to topics in this book. All of the sites on FactHound have been researched by our staff.

1. Visit *www.facthound.com*
2. Type in this special code: 140484919X
3. Click on the FETCH IT button.

Your trusty FactHound will fetch the best sites for you!

Index

Look for all of the books in the Amazing Science: Life Cycles series:

From Caterpillar to Butterfly: Following the Life Cycle
From Mealworm to Beetle: Following the Life Cycle
From Puppy to Dog: Following the Life Cycle
From Seed to Daisy: Following the Life Cycle
From Seed to Maple Tree: Following the Life Cycle
From Tadpole to Frog: Following the Life Cycle